KEVIN

why? why? why?

Who lends a helping beak?

Clare Oliver

This is a Parragon Book
First published in 2001

Parragon
Queen Street House
4 Queen Street
Bath BA1 1HE, UK

Produced by

David West ☆☆ Children's Books
7 Princeton Court
55 Felsham Road
Putney
London SW15 1AZ

British Library Cataloguing-in-Publication Data

A catalogue record for this book is available from
the British Library.

ISBN 0-75255-365-8

Printed in Italy

Designers
Axis Design, Aarti Parmar, Rob Shone,
Fiona Thorne

Illustrators
Sarah Lees, Stan Peach, Andrew Tewson (SGA)

Cartoonist
Peter Wilks (SGA)

Editor
James Pickering

CONTENTS

4 Why do fish go to school?

4 Where would you find a town of dogs?

5 Which insects are champion builders?

6 Who bathes in dirt?

6 Which fish goes to the cleaners?

7 Who lends a helping beak?

8 Who dances for a mate?

8 Which is the loudest animal on Earth?

9 Which animal breathes in Morse Code?

10 Who gift-wraps dung?

11 Who gives drinks cans to a mate?

11 Who locks horns for a mate?

12 Who plays follow-the-leader?

12 Where can you see over a million crabs?

13 When do seals come ashore?

14 Who rides in a crocodile's smile?

14 Who leaves their babies with a child-minder?

15 Which bird cooks its own eggs?

16 Where do dormice go in winter?

16 Can birds sleep as they fly?

17 Who digs in for winter?

18 Who hunts by heat?

18 Can bats see in the dark?

19 Who has an inbuilt compass?

20 Why do stoats do a dance?

20 Which turtle fishes with worms?

21 Who goes fishing at the bottom of the sea?

22 Why do ants keep creepy-crawlies?

22 What plays with its food?

23 Who is the fussiest eater?

24 Which crab packs a stinging punch?

24 Which beetle squirts poisonous gas?

25 Which caterpillar turns into a snake?

26 Who drops nuts from on high?

26 Who has a favourite stick?

27 Are dolphins as clever as us?

28 Which are the scariest fish?

29 Which is the most venomous snake?

29 Which insects can kill people?

30 When did cats move in with people?

31 Why do cowboys ride horses?

31 Which animals risk their lives for us?

32 Index

Why do fish go to school?

Lots of fish shoal together in groups called schools. There's safety in numbers, and individuals are less likely to be picked off by hungry hunters, such as sharks.

Where would you find a town of dogs?

Prairie dogs are a type of rodent, relatives of mice and rats, that live in the USA and Mexico. Millions may live together in underground 'towns'.

Which insects are champion builders?

In relation to their size, termites build bigger structures than any other creature. They use grains of soil as bricks, and their own spit as cement.

Termite mound

Prairie dogs

?Who bathes in dirt?

Zebras and horses love to take a dirt bath. The grit works through their hair and rubs off any dead skin, while the dust soaks up oil from their coat. Lots of other furry creatures take dirt baths too, including cats and dogs.

Zebras

Grouper

?Which fish goes to the cleaners?

The grouper fish that lives on coral reefs goes to a special cleaning station when it wants to get spruced up. Shrimps and tiny fish called wrasse clean the grouper by eating up any lice, fungus or dead skin.

Who lends a helping beak?

Oxpeckers in Africa help pick ticks off a rhino's face. The rhino sits quite still, even when the birds' sharp beaks are poking about around its eyes and nostrils. It works out well for everyone – the rhino gets rid of the itchy ticks, and the oxpeckers get a free meal.

Oxpeckers

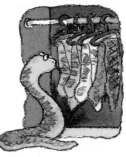

? Who dances for a mate?

A tree frog in Malaysia dances to attract his mate. The female can't see the dance, but she senses the movement of air as the male taps his feet.

Tree frog

? Which is the loudest animal on Earth?

The blue whale is the biggest living animal, and also the loudest. It can send messages to other blue whales that are over 500 km away!

? *Which animal breathes in Morse Code?*

Morse is a secret code made by mixtures of short and long signals. Rhinos seem to use a similar system to talk to each other. They string together special mixes of short and long breaths!

Rhinoceros

Blue whale

Cockatoos play drums.

TRUE. If a male cockatoo wants to impress a female, he holds a twig in his beak and beats a log.

Only a rattlesnake can rattle.

FALSE. Burrowing owls do, too. They rattle so that they sound dangerous, like rattlesnakes, to scare hunters.

Dung
beetle

❓Who gift-wraps dung?

❗Male dung beetles have a funny idea of what to give their girlfriend as a present – dung, to lay her eggs in. When the grubs hatch, they enjoy a smelly feast!

Who gives drinks cans to a mate?

Kea

The male kea displays red objects to impress his mate. He uses red flowers, buttons or even cola cans!

Reindeer

Who locks horns for a mate?

Lots of male animals fight over females. It's a way of showing off and also means that only the strongest get to mate. Reindeers fight by locking horns and pushing – that way, their bodies are less likely to get badly hurt.

Who plays follow-the-leader?

When it is time for a female echidna to mate, hopeful males queue up to be chosen! Up to ten male echidnas follow her, nose-to-tail.

Echidnas

Land crabs

Where can you see over a million crabs?

Every year, on Christmas Island in the Indian Ocean, millions of land crabs gather on the beach to lay their eggs. Each crab lays about 100,000 eggs!

Seals

? *When do seals come ashore?*

Although seals spend all their life in the sea, they come ashore to have babies. The seals leave their babies after a few weeks, though, because there's nothing for them to eat on the beach.

Crocodile and young

? Who rides in a crocodile's smile?

Crocodiles make very gentle mums. They carry their babies down to the river in their mouth – taking care not to bite them!

? Who leaves their babies with a child-minder?

Meerkats live together in large groups, or colonies. All the adults go out hunting during the day, leaving their babies in a nursery. One or two young adults are left behind to keep an eye on the little ones.

Meerkats

Mallee fowl

?Which bird cooks its own eggs?

The mallee fowl buries its eggs under an enormous pile of sand. The anxious dad keeps adding or taking away the sand so the eggs stay at a steady, toasty temperature.

TRUE OR FALSE?

Elephants often smack their calves.

TRUE. The grown-up elephants in a herd thump any badly-behaved baby elephants with their trunks.

Bear cubs live with their mum and dad.

FALSE. Daddy bear goes away before his cubs are born – mum looks after them alone.

15

❓ Where do dormice go in winter?

In autumn, dormice are busy feeding themselves up on nuts and berries. That's because they spend the winter underground, in nests. A lining of dry grass and leaves makes the nest soft and snug.

Dormouse

❓ Can birds sleep as they fly?

Swifts sometimes stay in the air for up to four years at a time, without ever landing. They don't just sleep in the air – they can drink, eat insects and mate on the wing, too!

Swift

? *Who digs in for winter?*

Bears sleep through the cold winter months, so they dig dens or stay in a cosy cave. They don't come out until the spring.

Bear and cubs

Pit viper

? Who hunts by heat?

The pit viper has an extra-special sense – it can detect heat. This helps it to find even the tiniest, best-hidden prey.

? Can bats see in the dark?

No, bats use sound, not sight, to find their way at night. The noise of their screeches bounces off objects so the bats can work out where they are, and what's around them.

Bat

Monarch butterfly

❓ *Who has an inbuilt compass?*

Monarch butterflies are the long-distance flight champs of the insect world. No one is certain how they find their way, but their bodies contain magnets, like a real compass.

TRUE OR FALSE?

Only bats use sound to find their way.

FALSE. Whales and dolphins use echoes to avoid bumping into things. This is called sonar – and submarines also use it!

Luna moths find their way by the Moon.

FALSE. They use feathery feelers to find their way, and can sniff out a mate many kilometres from them.

? Why do stoats do a dance?

To make rabbits curious! Stoats are very sneaky hunters. Once the rabbit comes near to see what on earth's going on, the stoat moves in for the kill.

Stoats

Alligator snapping turtle

? Which turtle fishes with worms?

The alligator snapping turtle has two fake 'worms' on the tip of its tongue. It wiggles the worms to tempt hungry fish to come near – and when they do, it gulps them down!

? Who goes fishing at the bottom of the sea?

The deep-sea angler fish feeds on other smaller fish, but it doesn't waste time and energy chasing them. Instead it has a 'fishing rod' to lure fish close to its mouth. It is very gloomy in the deep, so the 'rod' glows in the dark.

Angler fish

TRUE OR FALSE?

Snakes pretend to be worms.

TRUE. The end of the death-adder's tail looks like a juicy worm. When a bird flies down for it, the adder gobbles it up!

Birds catch fish with bread.

TRUE. Herons in Japan throw bread dropped by tourists into the lake. When the fish come to feed, the birds make their move.

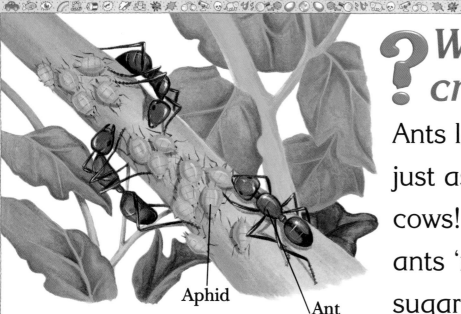

Aphid

Ant

?Why do ants keep creepy-crawlies?

Ants look after herds of aphids just as farmers keep dairy cows! The sweet-toothed ants 'milk' the aphids for the sugary liquid they produce.

?What plays with its food?

Killer whales play with seal pups before they eat them. No one knows why they toss the pups into the air. It could be to stun them, or it could just be for fun.

Koala

? *Who is the fussiest eater?*

The koala must be the fussiest creature on the planet. It will only eat eucalyptus, and sometimes it is so pernickety that it will only eat leaves from a particular tree!

Killer whale

TRUE OR FALSE?

Spiders' webs catch mice.

TRUE. Spider silk is super-strong, and also very sticky. Webs have caught mice and even small birds!

Leopards keep food in trees.

TRUE. They hunt large animals, and there's often too much to eat in one go. Leopards drag leftovers into a tree for later.

? Which crab packs a stinging punch?

Everyone knows that anemones sting, including the clever boxer crab. He holds an anemone in his two front pincers and soon sees off his enemies!

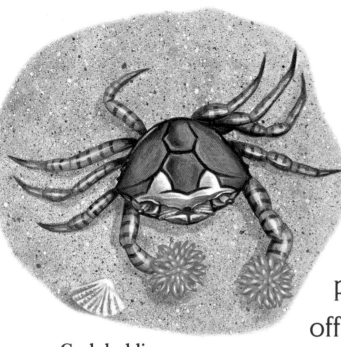

Crab holding anemones

? Which beetle squirts poisonous gas?

The bombardier beetle uses poison to frighten away would-be attackers. It squirts a jet of hot, toxic liquid out of its bottom! The jet makes a noise like a gun being fired.

Bombardier beetle

Hawkmoth caterpillar

❓ *Which caterpillar turns into a snake?*

One type of hawkmoth caterpillar makes itself look just like a tree snake when danger threatens. It shortens and thickens its head and turns over to reveal unblinking snaky 'eyes'. It even has a flickering 'tongue' to complete the scary disguise!

25

TRUE OR FALSE?

A head-dress scares enemies.

TRUE. The hawk-eagle has a crest of feathers that stand up, so the bird seems bigger and scarier than it really is.

Plovers pretend to be wounded.

TRUE. If an enemy comes near her nest, a plover pretends to be wounded and moves off to lure the enemy away.

Crow

? Who drops nuts from on high?

Clever crows often carry nuts in their beaks until they are flying over a hard surface, such as concrete. They drop the nut so that its shell smashes, and swoop down to gobble up the insides.

Chimpanzees

? Who has a favourite stick?

Chimps love to snack on crunchy termites, but their fingers are too short to winkle them from their mound. Instead, the brainy chimps carry a stick to use like a fishing rod.

Dolphins

?Are dolphins as clever as us?

Dolphins seem to talk to each other, and they learn tricks ever so easily, but humans are still the cleverest animals on Earth. We've learned how to read, write, build skyscrapers and do loads of other complicated things.

Piranhas

? Which are the scariest fish?

Sharks are the scariest fish in
the sea, but the scariest river fish are
piranhas. Piranhas have rows of razor-
sharp teeth and can strip a body down
to bare bone in seconds.

Mosquito

? Which insects can kill people?

Some people are frightened of wasps or earwigs, but the real insect baddie is the mosquito. It can carry malaria, a disease that kills more than a million people each year.

? Which is the most venomous snake?

Some sea snakes have venom that is 100 times more powerful than any other snake's.

Sea snake

? When did cats move in with people?

Cats first became tame in Ancient Egyptian times. They were wildcats, who came to hunt mice and rats living in the grain supplies. The Egyptians were so grateful that they even worshipped a cat goddess!

Sniffer dog

Why do cowboys ride horses?

People have ridden horses for thousands of years, in order to travel over huge stretches of land. Cowboys and gauchos ride so they can check on their cattle.

Which animals risk their lives for us?

Dogs are the bravest tame animals. They do all sorts of dangerous jobs for us. Sniffer dogs help search for bombs, or look for survivors after an earthquake. They also use their sense of smell to rescue people trapped in the snow after a mountain avalanche.

TRUE OR FALSE?

Dogs can do the laundry.

TRUE. Helper dogs do all sorts of tasks for their disabled owners, from bringing in the mail to loading the washing machine!

Camels can go without water for weeks.

TRUE. People often ride camels in hot places. The strong animals can carry goods across the desert, too.

Index

ants 5, 22

baby animals
14–15

bats 18

bears 15, 17

beetles 10, 24

blue whales 8, 9

butterflies 19

caterpillars 25

cats 6, 7, 17, 30

chimps 26

communication
8–9

crabs 12, 24

crocodiles 14, 29

crows 26

defence 24–25

dogs 6, 31

dolphins 19, 27

dormice 16

echidnas 12

fish 4, 6, 21, 28

food 20–23, 26

frogs 8

grooming 6–7

homes 4–5

horses 6, 31

keas 11

koalas 23

killer whales 22

mallee fowls 15

mating 10–13

meerkats 14

mosquitoes 29

piranhas 28

prairie dogs 4

reindeers 11

rhinos 7, 9, 13

seals 13

senses 18–19

snakes 7, 9, 21,
29

spiders 11, 13, 23

stoats 20

swifts 16

tame animals
30–31

termites 5

turtles 20

vipers 18

zebras 6